ENDA WALSH

Enda Walsh was born in Dublin
plays include a radical adaptatio
(Corcadorca, 1994), *The Ginger
Disco Pigs* (Corcadorca, 1996, then Traverse Theatre, 1997,
winner of the 1997 Stewart Parker Award and the 1997 George
Devine Award), *Sucking Dublin* (Abbey Theatre, Dublin, 1997;
winner of the 1997 George Devine Award), *Misterman*,
Bedbound (Royal Court Theatre Upstairs, 2001), *The Small
Things* (Menier Chocolate Factory, 2005), *Chatroom* (National
Theatre, 2005), *The Walworth Farce* (Druid Theatre, Galway,
2006, then Traverse Theatre, 2007; winner of Edinburgh Fringe
First Award, 2007), *The New Electric Ballroom* (Kammerspiele,
Munich, 2005, then Druid Theatre, Galway, and Traverse
Theatre, Edinburgh, 2008; winner of Theater Heute's Best
Foreign Play, 2005, Edinburgh Fringe First Award, 2008, Best
New Play, Irish Times Theatre Awards, 2008), *Delirium*, an
adaptation of Dostoevsky's *The Brothers Karamazov* (for
Theatre O, Abbey Theatre and Barbican, 2008), *Penelope*
(Traverse Theatre, 2010, then Hampstead Theatre, 2011; winner
of Edinburgh Fringe First Award, 2010). *Disco Pigs* and
Bedbound have been translated into eighteen languages and
have had productions throughout Europe.

His plays for radio include *Four Big Days in the Life of Dessie
Banks* for RTÉ, which won the IPA Radio Drama Award, and
The Monotonous Life of Little Miss P for the BBC, which was
commended at the Grand Prix Berlin. His 2008 biopic, *Hunger*,
told the story of the final days of IRA hunger striker Bobby
Sands and won awards including the Caméra d'Or at the Cannes
Film Festival and the Heartbeat Award at the Dinard
International Film Festival. It was nominated for seven BIFAs
(including Best Screenplay), six British Film and Television
Awards (including Best Screenplay and Best Independent Film)
and BAFTA's Outstanding British Film Award 2009.

Enda Walsh

MISTERMAN

NICK HERN BOOKS

London

www.nickhernbooks.co.uk

A Nick Hern Book

Misterman first published in the edition *bedbound and misterman* in Great Britain in 2001 as a paperback original by Nick Hern Books Limited, 14 Larden Road, London W3 7ST

Reprinted in this revised edition in 2012

Misterman copyright © 2001, 2012 Enda Walsh

Enda Walsh has asserted his moral right to be identified as the author of this work

Cover photo of Cillian Murphy by Richard Gilligan (www.richgilligan.com)
Cover design by Ned Hoste, 2H

Typeset by Nick Hern Books, London
Printed in the UK by Mimeo Ltd, Huntingdon, Cambridgeshire PE29 6XX

A CIP catalogue record for this book is available from the British Library

ISBN 978 1 84842 263 6

This version of *Misterman* was first produced by Landmark Productions and Galway Arts Festival, and performed at the Black Box Theatre, Galway, as part of the Galway Arts Festival, on 11 July 2011 (previews from 7 July). The cast was as follows:

THOMAS MAGILL   Cillian Murphy

WITH THE VOICES OF
MAMMY	Marcella Riordan
EDEL	Alice Sykes
OTHERS	Eanna Breathnach, Niall Buggy, JD Kelleher, Simone Kirby, Mikel Murfi, Morna Regan, Eileen Walsh, Barry Ward

Director	Enda Walsh
Designer	Jamie Vartan
Lighting Designer	Adam Silverman
Sound Designer	Gregory Clarke
Composer	Donnacha Dennehy

The production transferred to St Ann's Warehouse, New York, on 30 November 2011, and the Lyttelton auditorium of the National Theatre, London, on 18 April 2012 (previews from 14 April).

An earlier version of *misterman* was performed by Corcadorca Theatre Company at the Granary Theatre, Cork, in April 1999. The cast was as follows:

THOMAS MAGILL   Enda Walsh

Director	Pat Kiernan
Designer	Aedin Cosgrove and Mick Heffernan
Lighting Designer	Aedin Cosgrove
Sound Designer	Cormac O'Connor

Characters

THOMAS MAGILL

VOICES ON TAPE

SIMPLE EAMON MORAN
DWAIN FLYNN
MRS O'DONNELL
MAMMY
BILLY
MR McANERNY
MRS CLEARY
MRS HEFFERNAN
TIMMY O'LEARY
EDEL

*Pre-show and we're looking at an abandoned depot /
dilapidated factory. The space immediately feels
inhabitable and dangerous with electrical cables
everywhere. And yet dotted about it are small tiny
'stages', pristine in comparison to the surrounding debris.
It suggests that someone is trying to live and has lived
here for some time.*

The lights go down and fade back up.

*A thirty-three-year-old man is standing in the space facing
us, out of breath and sweating. This is* THOMAS. *He has
a small sliced pan under his arm. He stands upright and
opens his hand. He's holding a chicken's egg. It's a little
dirty. He must have taken it from a chicken coop.*

A dog can be heard barking outside the space. THOMAS
looks towards it.

*Suddenly Doris Day can be heard singing 'Everybody
Loves a Lover'.* THOMAS *turns, startled. He walks
quickly towards a tape recorder and picks it up. He hits
the stop button, but nothing. He unplugs it from the back
but the song continues. He takes out the batteries but
there's no stopping Doris. He places it down on the
ground like it was a bomb. He must try to ignore it. This is
most unusual.*

*The song continues as he walks into the kitchen space he's
made for himself, where he has a gas stove. He breaks the
egg into a little saucepan, adds some margarine and
leaves it there on a low heat. This bloody song.*

*He walks to a small basin with water and soap. He
vigorously washes his face and hands.*

When he finishes this, he leaves there, and walks back and stands looking over the wayward tape recorder and Doris. He's got an idea.

He walks quickly to the back of the space, bends down and picks up something. He walks back towards the tape recorder holding a hammer. He smashes it down on the tape recorder. The song skips back to the very start and remains intact.

THOMAS *petulantly screams with frustration.*

He covers his ears but can still hear it. He has some tissue in his hands. He tears it up and shoves it in his ears. It's no good. He takes off his jumper and wraps it around his head, covering his ears. Still no good.

He smells the egg cooking and returns to it fast. He turns up the heat and vigorously scrambles it. He empties it onto a slice of bread on a plate, and places it on a table.

But still this bloody song continues. He's got another idea. He disappears momentarily to a small room at the very back of the space. Sounds of pots and pans crashing to the floor.

When he returns out of the room, he's taped two dirty teddy bears over his ears. Perfect.

Happy now, he walks back to the tape recorder and stands over it.

It suddenly stops. Fuck it.

He rips off his teddy-bear mufflers and walks up some stairs that lead to a crumbling platform. Up there he sits behind a table with two reel-to-reels on it.

THOMAS. Hello, everyone!

He turns on both machines and gets to work.

We hear the voice of Simple Eamon Moran.

SIMPLE EAMON MORAN. Aren't ya talkin' to me any more? Why'd you run away from me garage…? No need for it.

THOMAS *fast-forwards it and stops it.*

… and will ya be goin' to the dance in the school hall tonight, Starsky?

THOMAS *fast-forwards it and stops it. We hear the voice of Dwain Flynn.*

DWAIN FLYNN (*screams*). Are you recordin' this? Once more for the record? You're not fuckin' wanted…!

He fast-forwards the tape again and stops.

And don't ever stand there!

THOMAS *stops the tape. Stands and looks to a spot beneath the platform. He impersonates Dwain.*

THOMAS. 'And don't ever stand there!'

He spits.

Good!

He sits and fast-forwards the tape. He stops and plays it. We hear the voice of Mrs O'Donnell.

MRS O'DONNELL. … and maybe it's best you went home.

THOMAS. Yes!

He's found what he's looking for. THOMAS *rewinds the tape and stops. We hear more of Mrs O'Donnell.*

MRS O'DONNELL. You've taken things too far. Jesus, look at your face – there's still blood – you need help, Thomas. Don't be goin' inside the hall. Maybe it's best you went home, love.

THOMAS stops both machines and stands up. He pauses and looks down at them momentarily.

He places the chair in a definite position. He then takes a tape recorder in a canvas sling and puts it over his shoulder, securing it to his belt like a holster.

Carefully he places a cassette tape in the machine. He pats it gently.

Quick now and THOMAS *comes back down the stairs.*

He walks over to a loudspeaker on the wall and takes the microphone.

He covers his eyes and...

Blackout.

In the darkness, THOMAS *is heard, his whisper amplified.*

THOMAS. It all began from a Nothing. This loud crashing all began as a whisper... but a whisper that was from God, from Him, from the Lord our Master... and that whisper grew and grew and became this growling and soon a thundering and a roaring that was never heard in the Nothing before. And out of the noise came a voice, the great voice of the Lord and He said, 'Let there be light'... and on the Nothing a light shone. And what was the first light like?

Lights slowly come up on all the small playing areas dotted about the space.

The light made the Nothing a Something which the Lord called Night and light was called Day. And He made the Earth and separated dry from wet to make the land and the sea, and He made vegetation and fruit and trees and covered the land in all colour and shone a bright yellow star to make the trees and plants grow. And then a universe of smaller stars and other planets He set turning in the speckled light. And animals of all kinds and shapes they ran about the Earth and swam in the lovely blue seas that as a child I too would swim in. And God made us, Daddy told me. Man and Woman in his likeness to keep watch on what He had made. To be watching. To be always watching. To be good.

THOMAS *is fully lit now, his hands lowered from his eyes as he talks into a microphone.*

But Man and Woman's soul was not like God's soul because it was good and evil. And evil it grew. It grew like that very first whisper but a whisper now of crying and suffering and it grew and is growing. And I'm watching… because more people fill the Earth and only some little good and some little happiness is found. Because Man has forgotten God's words He gave us in Eden… and His son, we crucified Him, we killed Him for offering us kind redemption and just carry on and on and on and sin has become our religion, greed our communion and Evil… Evil is our God.

He looks upwards.

(*Whispers up.*) Everything is not good, Daddy.

A pause.

He looks up at a light-blue suit hanging from chain that stretches all the way to the ceiling.

He then looks at his watch.

Four, three, two, one. Mammy!

He turns on the reel-to-reel on the table. Mammy is heard from it.

MAMMY. A scrambled egg is awful, Thomas? You used to take them boiled. What's the matter, my best boy in Ireland?

THOMAS. Tomorrow they'll be boiled again, Mammy. It's like eating yellow spit off a soggy bit of toast.

MAMMY. Stick with what ya know!

THOMAS. True enough, Mammy.

MAMMY. Something I learnt when I traded the Milk of Magnesia for those Gaviscon tablets. God, d'ya remember that?

THOMAS. Yes I do unfortunately.

MAMMY. Jaynee, I ate that many tablets that day I ballooned into the size of a whale only to expel myself in the evening for a good two hours.

THOMAS. There's a great honesty to Milk of Magnesia.

MAMMY. Milk of Magnesia's been clearing out foreign bodies for decades, hasn't it? It's like the United States of America of stomach medicines.

THOMAS *and Mammy laugh like fools.*

THOMAS. I thought I might visit Daddy at the cemetery. I got some blue lilacs and lined the rim of the grave. I got a new bit of that gravel green stuff as well and I made a map of Ireland with the green gravel. It looks like Ireland drowning on the grave with the terrible sea surrounding it.

MAMMY. Oh, that's nice! I think it's great you like flowers, Thomas. It's a nice side to your character.

THOMAS. It is, isn't it.

MAMMY. Are we all right for gas, Thomas? How's the canister?

THOMAS. The canister's fine, Mammy.

MAMMY. It's a little damp in here though…

THOMAS. Well, that's the dampeness for ya!

MAMMY. A certain draughtiness too.

THOMAS. There's a damp and certain draughty quality, all right.

MAMMY. There's no shifting it, is there?

THOMAS. No, there's no chance of that.

MAMMY. 'There's only living with it.' That's what you always say, isn't it, Thomas?

THOMAS. Well, who knows… ya might be blessed with a winning Lotto ticket… then you can buy all the gas canisters you want, Mammy. You could fill this whole room with that many canisters it would be like waking up in the Bahamas.

MAMMY. Ohhh, that would be nice.

Finishing his eggs. Closes his eyes and says a short prayer.

THOMAS. Lord, watch over your humble servant, keeping his soul clean, his spirit strong, through Christ our Lord, Amen. Right… best make a start!!

MAMMY. You might give me a rub with the Vicks when you get back from your travels?

THOMAS. I heard you coughing all night, d'ya know. It's not too good, Mammy. Like an old engine. Chugging away there, good style! Like a steam train, Mammy! Like a little old choo-choo!!

MAMMY (*laughing*). Oh, a little old choo-choo!

THOMAS. Like a choo-choo train from the olden days!

MAMMY. Choo-choo! Choo-choo! Choo-choo! Choo-choo! Choo-choo!

THOMAS. Ya got it, Mammy – that's right, Mammy –
that's enough now!!

Mammy stops laughing.

I'll give ya a rub-down later on, Mammy… don't you
worry about that.

MAMMY. Off with you then, Mister Traveller. Get me a
surprise from Centra, Thomas. A sugary surprise,
Thomas. You know what I like, love.

THOMAS. Oh, I know what you like. Bye now,
Mammy.

*He hits the play button on another reel-to-reel. He
unlocks some invisible locks on an invisible door. The
sound of the outside world from the recorder.*

THOMAS *'steps outside'.*

Car.

The sound of a car.

Dog.

The sound of a dog.

Billy.

BILLY. Howya, Thomas!

THOMAS. Hiya, Billy! (*Slight pause.*) I feel the front
door's gentle shove behind me as I step out into
Inishfree. My town. The Lord God at my side… the
day open and big!

He adopts a suitable voice for Mrs O'Leary.

'Oh the cold, Thomas!'

Are ya full of the cold, Mrs O'Leary?

'Once I get the cold into my body it's very difficult to get the cold out, Thomas. Try as I might, the cold just sits inside and won't budge an inch. And you, love, going out for your lil walk, are ya?'

I am! Off out for Mammy, actually. Got to keep her in the biscuits.

'Oh, she loves her biscuits, doesn't she!? She's mad about them biscuits!'

She loves her biscuits all right.

'A demon for the bicky, ya'd say!'

Well, not exactly a 'demon', Mrs O'Leary. There's a lot of contemplation that goes with old age. No harm that this quiet solitude is accompanied by the occasional Jammie Dodger.

'You're a fine son to her, Thomas! Oh, for God's sake, when I think of my own son, Timmy!'

A slight pause.

Well, what is it, Mrs O'Leary?

'Well, when I think of him with his disco nights and the way he'd bark at me like I was a black slave or something. "Mammy," he would shout! "MAMMY!" Like an old hound he would bark at me, Thomas. And I'd crawl in. Crawling into his bedroom because of these bunions stuck on my feet. I crawled into Timmy's bedroom the other evening and I'm not having ya on when I say a bomb had been let off… and then the smell, Thomas… Well, what with the bomb and then the smell…'

My God, was it terrible, tell me?

'Terrible isn't the word, Thomas! Beyond terrible! And he's sat there on his leaba like some lord, eating a large bowl of Sugar Puffs and playin' that awful computer game. I was scrubbing his room for days with my hands torn to shreds by the Harpic. Sure look at them!'

Well, that's not on, Mrs O'Leary! That's not on at all! Sure who brought us into the world only our mammies… 'Children, be obedient to your parents in the Lord'… that is what uprightness demands.

A sound of a car horn. THOMAS *gestures a hello.*

If you can't wake on the Lord's day and tidy away the odd pair of underpants, if it is not in your spirit to say that the spuds were lovely and that the meat was tender… if your parents are reduced to crawling around the house with calloused feet, well, in my book you're not even fit for pig-fodder. Look, you send Timmy around my way and I'll have a word in his ear.

A pause.

'D'ya know what I'd do if I didn't have my senses?'

I don't, Mrs O'Leary.

'I'd kidnap ya, ya little treasure!!'

Ahhh now, Mrs O'Leary, stop it!

(*Wistfully.*) 'No, I would, Thomas. That's what I'd do. The guards would have to lock me up for kidnappin' ya.'

God bless you, Mrs O'Leary, and don't you worry about Timmy.

He does a gesture to say goodbye to her but it's not right.

No!

He does the line again.

God bless you, Mrs O'Leary, and don't you worry about Timmy.

He gestures to her in a new way. That's correct.

Better.

He takes out a small notebook and writes.

'Timmy O'Leary. Cleanliness.'

Adopts the voice of Dwain Flynn.

'What are ya writing? You're writing in your little book again? Are ya writing about me this time? Are ya reporter, is that what it is? Reportin' about the community dance in the school tonight. Thomas Magill, the Inishfree Rovin' Reporter. Reporting to who exactly? Is it Denis Boyle? 'Cause he's a measly old fucker if ever there was one. The amount of drink I've had in there over the years! Hundreds I've spent in there – thousands!'

Impossible to put a figure on it, I'd say.

'Last weekend I spent me wages on pints only for Denis Fucking Boyle to turf me out… For what, says you? For fuckin' bad language he says!'

Well, I must commend Denis for his Christian actions.

'You agree with him then?'

Dwain smacks THOMAS *hard on the side of the head.*

I do agree with him wholeheartedly, yes!

'Sure where's the harm in the odd "fuck" or the occasional "ya dirty old cunt"! It's not written in the Bible that ya can't say those words, is it, Mr Holy Man?'

Those words wouldn't be written in the Holy Book, no, Dwain.

'Didn't they have those words in the Middle East?'

They did, Dwain, yes! And worse words I'd say those Arabs had! The reason why those words didn't feature in the Bible is because our Lord would want us to operate on a higher plain... Dwain? Not for human beings the language of dogs, the language of the dirty mutt. At our disposal are thousands of words which we can throw together in various patterns and create all manner of wonderful text and commun...

'Fuck you!'

A slight pause.

'Did you hear what I said, you fucking queer! Fuck you and your fucking words!'

A slight pause.

'Put that in your little book, you fucking headcase! And don't ever stand there!'

He spits.

THOMAS *watches Dwain walk off. He writes in his book.*

'Dwain Flynn. Profanity.'

THOMAS *cues Roger the dog.*

Roger!

Sound of little Roger barking.

Away, Roger! Get away!

The dog wanders off. Sound of car approaching and stopping. THOMAS *finds a chair and sits on it.*

He adopts the voice of the gloriously pompous Mr McAnerny.

'Dull ol' day, isn't it?'

(*Cheery.*) Well, it will brighten up hopefully!

'D'you think it will brighten up, Mister Weatherman?'

Well, it might, Mr McAnerny.

'I don't think it will, ya know.'

Well, it might or it mightened, who's to say?!

'I'd say you'd be better putting your money on the "mightened". I'd say that's where the wise money's going, Misterman.'

Well, whether it will rain or not… I suppose we'll see the outcome soon enough!

'Of course we'll see the outcome soon enough, ya can always count on that one. That's the thing with "time", you see. Wait around long enough and sure as eggs is eggs something is bound to happen.'

Mirror!

THOMAS *adjusts an invisible side-mirror on the invisible car.*

'Ah surety really that circumstances will be what they weren't due to the passing of time.'

That's right!

'A fool would bet against "time" having no effect on an event of some sort happening at some point. The very certainty of "time" continuing and proceedings altering due to the passing of minutes is a profundity that we live with daily.

In a nutshell, Thomas… "Time" changes everything. (*Slight pause.*) Goin' to the community dance in the school hall tonight then, young man?'

No – I wouldn't be one for the loud music, to be honest with ya.

MR McANERNY. So off on your little walk then?

THOMAS *surprised and annoyed by the intrusion of the voice from the tape.*

THOMAS. 'So off on your little walk then?'

I'm off to visit the cemetery, actually.

'Your poor dad. Now, he was great man. Great man. Best shop in town! What a variety! A selection! And for those days. I mean, bananas are two-a-penny now, of course! But back then when your dad was your age, sure people would travel to see the variety. Imagine saying that people would travel to see a banana. Sounds bonkers but that's the truth. That's the world's truth!! "Travelling to see a banana. That's where we're off to! We're off to see a banana from the jungles of Africa!!" Word would get around of the soft yellow fruit that was selling in Magill's Grocery and lines… I mean lines of people talking and laughing over this funny old bendy banana thing and all the people with the bendy banana grin on their old pusses, laughing and giggling away like happy monkeys!'

Toto's 'Africa' is playing on the radio.

'Oh yes!'

Mr McAnerny turns it up loud.

Yes! YES! TOTO!

THOMAS *stands listening to it for too long. He blocks his ears and turns away, the song muffled and fading out.*

I stop listening…

He looks up.

… and look up. I look up to where I want to be. Up there safe in the clouds and far away from Inishfree.

THOMAS *imagines himself in Heaven.*

I sit like an angel of goodness up here. Sit in the bluey-white making me invisible. I listen to God's music soothing and piercing me with His goodness. No more the smart words of Charlie McAnerny draining the life out of me. My head now free and without pain. (*Pause.*) I'm in a place where others' speak is like poetry too. A place where I belong. I see other faces surrounding me. Beautiful and kind they welcome Thomas. Angels all of us as we sit amongst the clouds. I have a look down on Inishfree. My town. (*Pause.*) And I see its pure white soul being stained by the bad. I see the goodness being chased out of people's faces. I look how temptation is twisting its ugly way into my neighbours… like they were blind and playing at the gates of Hell they look. But the good angel will make it change. My bright light of goodness making the pure grow again. And God has placed his hand around my shoulder. And me and God smile and look down on all my good work. 'It's going to be such a beautiful place, Lord. Such a beautiful place.'

A pause.

Again we hear Mr McAnerny from a reel-to-reel.

MR MCANERNY. Got to be off myself. See you, no doubt, in time.

THOMAS *takes out his notebook and writes.*

THOMAS. 'Charlie McAnerny. Immodesty.'

Suddenly the reel-to-reel begins to chew up with different voices layered over one another, making them intermittently unintelligible. THOMAS *stands looking at it, pissed off.*

It stops and clear as anything we can hear MR McANERNY *talking with* THOMAS.

MR McANERNY. I'm saying it for your own good, all right? Do you hear me, Thomas?

A slight pause.

THOMAS (*on tape, whispered*). Yes.

MR McANERNY. This behaviour has to stop. (*Slight pause.*) Now, if you ever need to…

THOMAS *stops the reel-to-reel.*

A sudden noise from outside the space. It's that dog whimpering and wanting to be let in.

THOMAS (*screams at it*). Go away!

He barricades the door with a huge piece of furniture.

Silence now. The dog has wandered off.

Good!

THOMAS *races across the space to a new playing area, as he goes over a line of Simple Eamon Moran's.*

'But they're creepy old places, aren't they, Thomas?!'

THOMAS *turns on another reel-to-reel. The sound of birds twittering and the outside. He adjusts the volume but it goes too loud. He blocks his ears and hammers the top of the machine. It finds the correct volume.*

He pulls back a large piece of plywood. Behind it is a structure full of crosses made out of cans of Fanta.

THOMAS *grabs a handful of flowers, composes himself, and checks his watch.*

Four, three, two, one. Gate.

The sound of a gate opening as THOMAS *enters the cemetery to visit his daddy's grave.*

Hello, Daddy, it's only me, Thomas. I just popped out to get the mammy the bickies – I thought I'd check in with ya. (*Slight pause.*) The grave's looking smashing, by the way! It's the best of the lot, I'd say! Hey, what do you make of the gravel map of Ireland on the drowning sea? It's dynamite, isn't it, Daddy?! A good joke. A-one!

THOMAS *kneels down at his daddy's grave and lays the flowers on it.*

So! Mickie-Joe-Goblin-McAllister's been banned from the community centre for life, Daddy. A physio woman from out of town had a weekend clinic for the elderly. There was all manner of crippled people queuing down the road to avail of her healing hands. I had thought of bringing Mammy but she said she'd feel very awkward about another woman feeling her up. Not so Mickie-Joe. Apparently he walked in, dropped his knickers, said he had a chest infection and might he have a suck of a lozenge.

A slight pause.

He's not half as funny as he makes himself out to be. In my mind he's just a grubby little midget with a very long name – though that can go a long way in Inishfree, unfortunately organ.

The sound of a church organ playing 'Lord of All Hopefulness'.

Billy Traynor got himself a new car, Daddy! Who's to say there's no money in shovelling S-H-I-T! He's as proud as punch just like the fella on the Lotto ad! Hey, will ya ever forget the day ya caught him pinching the newspaper in our shop, Daddy? Ya gave him an awful

hiding that day! He was in bits that night in Boyle's!
Pouring the pints inta him to ease the pain! Billy's only
an old thief anyway! Everyone knows that. No doubt
he'll be at the dance tonight, jangling those new car
keys at the young girls, God help them.

A pause.

I really miss ya, Daddy. But I'm doing my best with it
and I bet you'd be proud of the work I'm doing about
town too. It's just funny not having the shop... and it
being so quiet about the house with Mammy and me
and Trixie. The swelling's gone down after the kittens,
by the way. Mammy asked me to drown three of them
and keep the best one. 'Best to drown the lot,' I said.
Being an only child is tough... being an only kitten in a
town full of dogs would be a terrible curse though. It
really would.

THOMAS *listens to the 'Lord of All Hopefulness'*
moving through the air around him. He begins to sing.

Lord of all kindness,
Oh oh, Lord of all grace,
Your hands swift and welcome,
Your arms... they embrace,
Be there... for my mammy,
And give us... to pray,
Your love is in my heart, Lord,
At the break of the day...

THOMAS *adopts the voice of Simple Eamon Moran.*

'But they're creepy old places, aren't they, Tommy?
Gives me the creeps just working beside the thing.'

Oh, Eamon! Well, what's creepy to some, gives great
comfort to others. Though Daddy's sitting upstairs with
the Almighty, down here his grave and remains still
nourish my soul.

'God, he was a great man though, wasn't he?'

You wouldn't be able to call many people great but my daddy was great, all right.

'And strong too! You wouldn't want to cross your daddy. He could crush walnuts with his little finger, couldn't he, Tommy?'

'There wasn't a walnut safe in Inishfree,' he used to say.

A slightly uncomfortable pause as THOMAS *waits for an invitation from Eamon.*

'Will ya have a cup a tea with me? I've got the kettle on in the garage.'

Well, that's awfully Christian of you, Eamon!! Just... wait a sec!

THOMAS *turns off the cemetery reel-to-reel, grabs a chair and quickly sets up Eamon's garage space. He turns on a reel-to-reel inside there. Sound of music.*

'There's very little things as good as tea in my book. Sure tea is what's made this country great!'

He fills two cups with a two-litre bottle of Fanta.

'And even if it isn't great, at least we have tea to help us through the terrible darkness.'

We do that. Tea's a great salve.

A big dog is heard growling.

Good Lord, that's a very big dog!

'That'll be Rufus, he's harmless, him. Loves the rabbits but very good with the kiddies.'

Oh, right.

'So grab a seat where ya can! Hope ya like your tea strong. Me, I like my tea like tar. Unless ya can trod on the stuff it's useless to me, boy!'

Sure once it's wet and warmish it's no bother to me! Well, Slàinte mhath!

'Go bhfana í ngrá linn,
Iad siúd atá í ngrá linn.
Iad siúd nach bhfuil,
Go gcasa Dia a gcroíthe.
Agus muna gcasann Sé a gcroíthe
Go gcasa Sé caol na coise acu
Go n-aithneoimid iad as a mbacadaíl.'

THOMAS *has no idea what Eamon said.*

Oh, very good. (*Slight pause.*) My God, what a collection of cars you've got here! But ya know, Eamon… I can't see the attraction in travelling at all! People whizzing around from A to B and not spending enough time having a good look around! Do you know what I mean?

'I don't, Tommy, but ya plan ta tell me all the same!'

Ah, I won't go boring ya now, Eamon!!

THOMAS *laughs. Eamon laughs. They laugh together.* THOMAS *continues.*

It's just… it seems to me at least… that people are filling their lives with unnecessary entertainment when the Lord has provided everything that is needed already right there on their doorstep. If time wasn't always spent in life's fast lane, people would see the simple beauty of the Lord. Now you know what I mean by that, don't you?

'No.'

Well, don't you worry that one day you'll wake up and
forget about all what the Lord has done for you? That
the sunrise and the changing seasons won't surprise
you any more? We were given such a great gift, Eamon,
and such a beautiful and wonderful world to play in.
It's this arrogance that some people have. This wasting
of everything.

From somewhere, THOMAS *has found a hurley.*

All the Lord wants is us to love Him as He loves us. To
return His love and to love each other. Why is that so
difficult, Eamon? (*Slight pause.*) When the Lord is not
the first thing in your life, it is not a life. Love and
respect the Lord God and Heaven will be your eternal
home. It's that simple.

'You're a walking saint, Tommy! The whole town's
saying it, by Jaynee!! No doubt about it but you're well
touched.'

Touched?

'By the man Himself is what I mean!'

Oh, right.

THOMAS *has found a kindred spirit.*

Well, a prophet of God needs a following, Eamon.
Look, I understand that you've got your hands full here
in the garage here and helping out with the hurling
team at the weekends, but I've always felt that you've
understood… that you understand my work in the town
here… that there's a bond, maybe, between us. If you
were to work alongside me – now I would work you
hard but fair. We would call on people together. Put
right where there is wrong. Comfort where there is
loneliness. God's work is tough but the rewards,
Eamon, are so great, ya know!

'I'd have to talk it over with the lads in the hurling team 'cause I wouldn't want to take the Lord's work lightly. I'd put in one hundred per cent for the Man Upstairs, you know that.'

We would be a great team, Eamon!

'We would, Tommy! We would! Crusaders is what we'd be!'

Well, exactly!

'Like Starsky and Hutch… except delivering God's Law, of course!'

(*Laughing.*) Oh, very good! Very funny, Eamon! Really great joke!

THOMAS *laughs and hammers the hurley on the ground.*

He cues Eamon on the reel-to-reel.

Eamon!

SIMPLE EAMON MORAN. Y'all have a hot sup, then, Starsky?!

THOMAS. I will, Hutch! Lash it in there, Eamon!! Thank you. God bless ya, partner!

A very long pause as THOMAS *and Eamon laugh quietly to themselves at their hilarious banter.*

Quietness then as THOMAS *looks around the garage.*

The atmosphere suddenly changes as he sees something pinned to the wall.

Is that what I think it is?

SIMPLE EAMON MORAN. Ah, don't be looking at that, Tommy.

THOMAS. But that, Eamon… that is filth. How any woman can strip off and allow that sort of… (*Slight pause.*) And… and you? You get satisfaction from some dirty prostitute stuck to your wall! Well, this is not good, Eamon! I took you as my colleague and not some sick pervert man! But guess who's been led on the big merry-go-round!! Who's the big eejit, only Thomas Magill!!

SIMPLE EAMON MORAN. Sure where's the harm in a calendar?!

THOMAS. 'Where's the harm?'!! Is it not Satan's Black Angel right in front of me then! Well, stop the rot – stop the rot!! Before I know it, you'll all be at it! Let me out of here!?

SIMPLE EAMON MORAN. Ah, Tommy, for crying out loud…!

THOMAS. My name is Thomas!! My name is Thomas! My name is Thomas! My name is Thomas!

THOMAS *smashes up the garage as Eamon's music blares out.* THOMAS *runs from the space.*

Dramatic lighting change as the music and THOMAS *stop.*

And I run! And run fast up over the hill and past the church! My good words sent burning about me. Inishfree once more all bad and diseased. My legs unable to climb to Heaven are stuck still in the Devil's land. In Sodom, good Christ! In Sodom! And run, Thomas, run! Turn back and see Simple Eamon Moran standing at his garage door… his eyes a piercing red, his ragged wings lit by fire!! (*Screams out.*) Lord God take me by my hand and lead me out of this festering pit! This Hell!! Save me, Lord, and place me sitting by Your side! Save me, Lord Almighty!! Save me!!

A dog starts barking on the reel-to-reel.

THOMAS *stops. He imagines the dog approaching him. He's terrified and slowly backs away.*

The dog is faded up to very loud now.

AWAY FROM ME, ROGER! GET HOME, ROGER! GET HOME!

THOMAS *freaks out with punches and kicking. He's killing the dog. The dog stops barking as he is knocked unconscious.* THOMAS *continues punching him.*

THOMAS *eventually stops.*

Music here.

THOMAS *stands upright. His knuckles are bleeding a little. He must have punched the ground. He washes his hands in the sink.*

He walks over to a new space where a small table and chair are set up.

He disappears from view momentarily into a small office room and reappears carrying a clean red-gingham tablecloth. He carefully places it on the table.

He turns on another reel-to-reel.

He sits. Music cuts.

Sound of a quiet café.

It wouldn't be every day that I'd give myself a treat like this one, but today I'm having a cheesecake! Definitely! Mrs Cleary's Café… the red-chequered tablecloths all bright and breezy. (*Whispers to himself, barely audibly.*) Cheesecake. Cheesecake. Cheesecake. Cheesecake. Cheesecake. Cheesecake. Cheesecake. Cheesecake. Cheesecake. Cheesecake. Cheesecake.

Cheesecake. (*Louder now.*) Cheese? And cake? How anyone could think that a whisked bit of cheese with a broken-biscuit base could set the baking world on fire... they must have been – (*Introducing.*) And here she is!! The Ban an ti!

THOMAS *spins up from his seat and grabs an overflowing battered kettle as samba music kicks in. He puts on the voice of the sultry Mrs Cleary.*

'Ahh, Thomas, but you're looking fabulous! What a rig-out! It's top, it really is!! Oh, look at ya! Jesus, ya've grown up to be a fine-looking fella! Best catch in Inishfree, I'd say! Ladies, are ya all right for the tea? Yee are!! That's fabulous that is and isn't Mrs Heffernan looking like a new model with her hairdo done up on her head like a hairy fairy cake, if there is such a thing, Thomas!! A hairy fairy cake? Not in my little café! Not on your nelly, oh no!! Wooooooo, would ya look at his lovely neat feet! Stuck there in his little shoes! I bet you're a dancer, hey, Thomas! I bet you're a dancer? Fred Astaire had feet the picture of those fellas! Grab a hold of Mrs Cleary and we'll have an old waltz for ourselves!'

I've just come in for a cheesecake, Mrs Cleary!

'And you've no time for a dance with me!? Are ya shy? You're not shy, are ya!? Sure that's a nonsense! Up and we'll have a turn around the floor! Tonight's the community dance, Thomas! We'll get in some practice and show the whole town in the school hall, won't we?! We'll show those old codgers a little bit of Fred and Ginger's still going strong as ya like in sad old Inishfree. Of course it is, ya little dancer!! Dancing dancing, ohhh, the little dancer dancing there in his dancing leprechaun dancing shoes!!'

The samba music cuts.

Look, if you don't mind!! I mean, if it's all right with you, I'd rather not dance here or in the hall this evening, you know! I was just out on my little walk to get Mammy the biscuits and I've just called in for some cheesecake! I mean, if it's all right with you, Mrs Cleary, I'd like a bit of your fabulous cheesecake. If that's all right now, Mrs Cleary!

Not impressed, and Mrs Cleary wanders off.

Ya can't be allowed to be seen dancing in the Mrs Cleary's Café… least of all with Mrs Cleary. Ya can never tell if the rumours are true but if they are there's quite a few farmers around Inishfree who've taken to the old whisked cheese and broken-biscuit base.

THOMAS *takes out his notebook and writes.*

'Mrs Cleary. Indecent.'

THOMAS *suddenly looks completely exhausted. He rests his head on the table for a good twenty seconds.*

MRS CLEARY. Your cheesecake, Thomas.

A real slice of cheesecake appears from beneath the table.

THOMAS (*brightly*). Thanks very much, Mrs Cleary! Magnificent… magnificence!

As THOMAS *eats his cake a conversation is heard on the reel-to-reel.*

MRS HEFFERNAN. … Oh, a little ways down from the garage. It was lying in the middle of the road.

MRS CLEARY. And whose is it?

MRS HEFFERNAN. The O'Donnell's, I think.

MRS CLEARY. Oh, little Roger?

MRS HEFFERNAN. Must have been hit by a car. It's dangerous there…

MRS CLEARY. Oh, it is, yeah. Oh, the poor little doggie.

The sound of a door being opened and a bell sounding.
THOMAS *turns to the reel-to-reel.*

Music.

Immediately he is mesmerised at what he sees.

THOMAS. And then something walks into my life. A vision with pale skin and her eyes green. She smiles at me as her dress blue brushes by my hand. By the back of my hand. I feel the tiny hairs on my fist tickle and stretch out, ya know the way they do. She catches my look sending me blushing and turning away. An angel, Thomas! A real angel. Jaynee, I feel weak all of a sudden. My back to her. Almost resting to her. I feel ashamed then. Can't figure out why – her grace and beauty, I suppose. So beautiful and pure. I listen to her at the counter. The life in her voice. The ease and humour of God's words. Only her words, sounding of summer sunshine. (*Pause.*) And then I see Eamon Moran's grubby hands… as large and gluttonous as that whore Mrs Cleary. In front of this angel everything is filth. Everything, Thomas.

He tries to clean the invisible filth from his hands with the tablecloth.

He suddenly looks up and she is standing beside him.

Hello. (*Slight pause.*) Thomas, that's right. (*Slight pause.*) When did you arrive? (*Slight pause.*) No, I haven't seen you. (*Slight pause.*) Well, I've been busy too. (*Slight pause.*) Doing my work, that's right? (*Slight pause.*) Yes, I'm doing my best. (*Slight pause.*) You've seen. Right. (*Slight pause.*) Yes, of course I'll follow.

THOMAS *leaves with the angel, the bell sounding again.*

The music continuing.

She walks towards the girls standing at the corner. The dust in the air, everything it glows. And Heaven has found its way to our grey withered old town and turned it all to Technicolor. And those smart-talkin' girls drop their stubby cigarettes and genuflect in front of her. They fall to their knees, bow their heads and she lays her hand over them and turns to me... and smiles.

He walks into the street and towards her.

And it's like I'm stepping into the bluey-white of the clouds all over again but with her by my side now. And I'm seeing an Inishfree being altered by her hope. Goodness transforms and the Lord God unlocks a beauty inside all these people... and neighbours greet one another with kind words... and community and respect is made by her just being here. (*Pause.*) 'You will not be alone any more, Thomas. Because today I will find you... and I will walk with you.'

His eyes fill with happy tears.

Thank you.

He smiles.

And from beneath her blue dress... and stretching out in the warmth of a new afternoon... wings. She takes to the sky and Heaven-bound she turns back to me. (*Slight pause.*) In vocation we are together, we are the same soul, me and you, the same One, that same smile! But what do I call you, Angel?! (*Pause.*) 'Edel.' Edel. Edel.

The music continues for some time as he watches her fly off.

The music cuts abruptly.

He does the nasty voice of Mrs O'Donnell.

'And what has you all pleased with yourself? You should be ashamed. I knew when I heard it. Mrs Cleary said it wasn't possible but when Simple Eamon Moran told me what you did out on the road. You punched him to bits. He's fucking dead, Thomas! Look at him! To see little Roger's body tipped on the side of the road like old rubbish. When my Marty hears what you've done he'll knock twelve shades of shit right out of you, believe me, boy! Are you listening to what I'm saying, you mad fucking eejit!?'

I am listening, Mrs O'Donnell, but to be honest you're making very little sense! Sure wasn't it your dog who took the first bite?

'But to kick the poor creature to death! Good Christ, man!'

Nobody is as sorry as me, Mrs O'Donnell! But in fairness it was either my boots or the vet's gun! It made little difference! The poor doggie didn't have a bright future once he bit me, now be honest, did he? I'll take these Jammie Dodgers off ya now, Mrs Pearson!

A packet of Jammie Dodgers drop from the sky into his hands.

Would love to talk to you, Mrs O'Donnell, but just have to get back to Mammy!

A slight pause.

I watch Mrs O'Donnell carry her wet tears down the road and disappear into the grey. And take a deep breath, feeling my soul lighten and ease once more.

The sound of wind swirling.

And that's when it starts, ya know! Those grey clouds gather above and start to spin… and Edel starts spinnin' them for my entertainment! And she spins them so fast I feel almost sucked up by them! Like I'm being sucked up by a giant Hoover and sent to somewhere beautiful! Somewhere where me and my angel walk hand in hand! Somewhere good, Thomas!

Enormous sounds and music as THOMAS *closes his eyes as his universe spins around him.*

The music and sounds continue for some moments.

They suddenly stop.

A voice on the reel-to-reel now. It's Mrs O'Donnell.

MRS O'DONNELL. … Is it true though? Did you really kill him, Thomas?

The samba music begins to blare out.

THOMAS (*on tape, whispering*). I don't know. I was on the road… I wanted to get away… (*Trails off. He can't talk.*)

He smashes off the café reel-to-reel but the other reel-to-reel suddenly mashes up and distorts.

It fixes itself and the sound now of THOMAS *running away and crying.* THOMAS *glares over at the reel-to-reel.*

He walks to it and turns it off.

He goes to the sink and cleans his hands again. He dries them and walks over to the space where he's made his mammy's kitchen.

He puts on the reel-to-reel on the kitchen table. Sound of generic country music is heard from a radio.

*He takes a can of Fanta from somewhere. He opens it
and drinks it back. It's a well-earned drink.*

MAMMY. Welcome back, the Thirsty Traveller! Would
you believe it but Trixie's in one of her moods again,
Thomas!

THOMAS. Is she now.

MAMMY. I threw her a frozen fish finger to lift her
spirits. She's been sucking on it like a fat cigar for a
good half-hour but you've never seen such a miserable
expression on a kitty.

THOMAS. Right.

MAMMY. She's just not been the same since all her
kitties got drowned.

THOMAS. Mammy, I've told you those kittens are in a
better place! You can't walk ten yards in Inishfree
without meeting a hound. (*To Trixie.*) Up, Trixie,
come on!

THOMAS *holds 'Trixie', a cat made of old jumpers.*

MAMMY. They say a dog can sniff out the bad in people.

THOMAS. Oh, do they now?

MAMMY. I read an article in *Ireland's Own* about doggie
intuition.

THOMAS. Well, sure it's no wonder the streets are
riddled with dogs so, when you think of the terrible
carry-on in this town!

MAMMY. Oh, very good!

THOMAS (*to Trixie*). Now, Mrs Trixie. 'Less you want to
end up in my notebook, you need to change your ways,
ya hear me now! Cheer up!

THOMAS *tosses Trixie away. Sound of a cat squealing on the tape.*

Time to take your top off, Mammy!

THOMAS *lifts up an enormous tub of Swarfega. He opens it and begins to massage it into the table. We can hear Mammy groan for some time. She stops.*

The sound of swirling wind again.

The Vicks begins to lift little clouds of doubt that often wander into my head. And I can see the happy destiny of Inishfree being painted by me and the Angel Edel. It's all beginning to turn. Goodness has found a new strength. And so the change begins.

THOMAS *continues to massage the Swarfega into the table. He stops and dries his hands.*

MAMMY. Thanks, Thomas! You're a great little healer. Great healing hands, God bless them.

THOMAS. Well, you know, sitting over a gas heater doesn't help your breathing, Mammy, I've said it once and I'll be saying it a thousand times.

MAMMY. Oh, but it gets awfully cold, Thomas.

THOMAS. I think you'll find that putting on some extra clothes will sort you out there. It doesn't take a brainbox to figure that one out, Mammy.

MAMMY. I'm sorry, Thomas.

THOMAS. All I'm asking you to do is throw on an extra jumper. It's not like I'm asking you to fetch me a packet of biscuits from the shop every day.

MAMMY. All right, Thomas.

THOMAS. Look, Mammy, I think a little more understanding is needed here. I'm looking after both our interests. Your sore cough and me wasting God's good time spreading the Vicks on. I'm asking you to do something that even you could manage, Mammy! A jumper, that's all! An extra jumper! Give me one less thing to be worried about.

MAMMY. Oh, I'm sorry…

THOMAS. I mean, do you have any idea of the day I've put down? And what now the Lord has bestowed on me! A little bit more cooperation would be appreciated! It would make my work a lot easier to come home to a happy home, Mammy! I'm not asking for much… but when I come through that door… what I expect… what I am looking for… is respect from you and Trixie. The same respect that you both showed Daddy…

MAMMY. Why, Thomas?

THOMAS. Ahhh, Mammy – you're not being very bright today, are ya? Do I have to spell it out to you?

MAMMY. Stop it, Thomas…!

THOMAS (*screaming*). You stupid woman! Have you understood anything I have said?! Just put on an f-ing jumper!

Music here.

Have you any idea of the cost of heating this room!? The f-ing gas bill, Mammy!! You will not ruin my work, woman!! Are you listening to me?! Look – JUST DO IT!!

Dogs outside have started to bark, seemingly startled by THOMAS *screaming.*

THOMAS *looks towards the metal door to the outside.*

(*Shouts.*) Come on then – HOUND!

He races to the door and smashes it with his fist. The dog goes crazy. THOMAS *starts smashing the door and barking back at the dog.*

MAMMY (*crying*). What are we going to do now, Thomas? What are we going to do…

The music and the dogs swell. THOMAS *turns back into the huge space he has created. A sudden power surge and the space is calling him back.* THOMAS*'s head drops as the music, dogs, lights continue aggressively.*

Suddenly he walks up to the 'street' reel-to-reel and turns it on. THOMAS*'s demeanour, bright and excited now, as he opens those invisible locks in the invisible door.*

Music suddenly stops. The sound of the outside, the sounds of a bright summer's day.

THOMAS. Car.

The sound of car.

Dog.

The sound of dog.

Billy.

BILLY. Howya, Thomas.

THOMAS. Hiya, Billy. (*Slight pause.*) I feel the front door's gentle shove behind me as I step out into Inishfree. My town. (*Slight pause.*) I look above and I see a bright light cut through the clouds. See her wings split the air. And she's coming now. She's here. (*Slight pause.*) Hello, Edel.

The reel-to-reel beside him suddenly begins and the voice of Timmy O'Leary is heard.

TIMMY O'LEARY. All right, Thomas.

THOMAS. Well, if it isn't Timmy O'Leary, the boy who treats his mammy like an old dog!

TIMMY O'LEARY. You what?

THOMAS. Slovenly behaviour will always catch up on a man, Timmy. Only this morning I listened to a litany of exploitation perpetrated on your little dote of a mammy.

TIMMY O'LEARY. What are you talkin' about?

THOMAS. 'What are you talkin' about? What's he talkin' about?' Do you hear this, Edel?! I'm talkin' about a sixty-seven-year-old woman crawlin' about on her hands and knees 'cause her feet are being eaten by bunions, Timmy!! A woman whose Harpic-poisoned hands have been mummified into tiny claws! Those same claws have to scoop up soiled underpants and toxic socks and all manner of fungaled food and all the time lorded over by her sullied son!

TIMMY O'LEARY. Are you with him?

THOMAS. She is with me, as a matter of fact, yes, but it's me talkin' to you, young man!

TIMMY O'LEARY. Right.

THOMAS. Right! Thirty-two years ago the Lord God planted a seed inside your mammy and gave your daddy the direction and drive to water that seed and thus began your foetal life inside your mammy's tummy. And she kept you there and no doubt gave you the proper nourishment a mother gives to her unborn child. She would have to endure atrocious heartburn, embarrassing flatulence, seismic swings in her personality, but she endured all of this, Timmy, out of love. And when she pushed you out in the Regional

Hospital there was probably not a happier woman in the whole of the county. And she brought you up, didn't she, and she watered and fed ya, and put clothes on your back and taught you how to read and write and introduced Jesus Christ through the catechism to you. She had hopes for you, Timmy! Happy hopes full of possibilities! And pictures, naturally, would form in your mammy's head as she filed her bunions of an evening! Amazing happy pictures of her son finding employment and putting his stamp on the world! And there, under God's direction, he would find a girl and suddenly your mother is choosing her rig-out for the 'big day', the many hats she could choose, Timmy! And yet only moments into your adult life it's like you're shrinking the world around you! And for each second you're living like this you are mocking the world that God has created, you are standing on the dreams of your mammy, you are denying her a son that she can be proud of – you are denying her fancy hats, Timmy!! (*Slight pause.*) Now will you do me a favour and think of that the next time you stand in your dirty bedroom?!

A slight pause.

TIMMY O'LEARY. Think of all of it?

THOMAS. Like a gospel of faith, think of it.

A pause.

TIMMY O'LEARY. Okay, Thomas, I have to go to the shops.

A pause.

THOMAS. Well, thanks very much, Edel. (*Pause.*) Oh, I do my best, you know. (*Pause.*) Well, to be honest I still believe this town could be great one day – all the nastiest words in the world couldn't turn me from my work. (*Slight pause.*) I always had God as a companion. Could always see Him in everything and everywhere just like that first prayer book tells you, you know. I can maybe sound too strong at times but the quicker we atone for our sins the sooner the world will open with love and peace...

She has said something.

What's that...? Well, yes... I'll go where you want. Just wait...

He grabs an old rolled-up battered green carpet. He places it on the ground and kicks it out. It unrolls majestically.

A pause as he 'watches' her lead the way.

We walk.

Music here.

And it's like the first walk. And around us good neighbours stop and bow their heads and let us pass, their souls rising up to Heaven then. Walk on and curtains twitch but with no laughter now, a grace is laid out before us and people will talk of this day for ever. Around us the shops and houses of Inishfree they slide beneath the ground and soon too the road falls beneath until all that's left is a blank horizon stretching on. And me and the Angel walk alone over a wilderness of dirt and lose ourselves in dreams of a better life. And there's only us in this world but already beneath our shoes a new grass begins to grow. And it grows underneath and spreads out over the wilderness – meadow of green and yellow crocuses pinging out of this carpet and stretching to a new sun in this new day. We walk on and about us an orchard pushes itself up from the earth. She talks God's words to me and about these words apples pop into life, ripen in moments and colour this green world with wonderful dots of red. How beautiful this new world is. How pure in hope, how free in dream. (*Slight pause.*) And the past history of me and what I have lived through, the hurt, the beatings, the abuse, the lies… they evaporate in the air around me. And we will build anew, her and me, and it will survive past a week and into years and centuries and we will make new histories of hope and peace and love.

The sound of a river now.

The orchard sweeps down to a river and our legs take us there, our hearts caught in anticipation. We find a clearing on the bank, the grass all soft beneath my hands and we sit and watch the blue-grey river moving past us.

He goes to her and sits. A pause.

I can see her wings all folded and white and soft they look. (*Slight pause.*) You've travelled so far, haven't you, Edel? (*Slight pause.*) And she smiles at me and stays quiet. We know what we are building. Our words have been said and now is the time to sit quietly in the Eden we've built.

A pause.

Her hand is stretched out on the grass.

A pause.

She's saying words I can't hear. (*Pause.*) Edel… can I hold your hand?

Thunder and the sound of torrential rain. The stage and THOMAS *are drenched in water from the fire sprinklers.*

THOMAS *stands up, furious and hurt.*

Not for the first time, God roars down on Inishfree! I walk in the rain with its tracks pouring down my face and drenching my heavy soul. I hear someone bark and then laugh! Laughing at me!! Will I ever be free from those laughs?! Walk on, Thomas!

Crash of thunder.

I'm feeling the whole town sit hard on my back and wanting to drag me down to their level. 'God saw that human wickedness was great on Earth and that human hearts contrived nothing but wicked schemes all day long. God regretted having made human beings on Earth and was grieved at heart. And God said, "I shall rid the surface of the Earth of the human beings whom I created – human and animal, the creeping things and the birds of Heaven – for I regret having made them." But Noah won God's favour. Noah was a good man, an upright man among his contemporaries, and Noah walked with God.'

Again a crash of thunder. THOMAS *starts barking at the whole of the town. He stops.*

I see some man outside my house with his thumb stuck to the doorbell, his face furious from the long wait and Mammy sat inside like the Queen herself! (*Laughs.*) He turns and walks fast towards me, yelling about his dead dog Roger! It's me he wants, it's me he wants!! Oh Christ, please, no!! No no NO!! DON'T DON'T!!

THOMAS *is struck on the face and falls to the ground. He splashes violently on the soaked ground, screaming like a child.*

Sound of Mr O'Donnell screaming at him from a reel-to-reel.

MR O'DONNELL. YOU FUCKING FREAK! TO KILL MY FUCKING DOG! YOU'RE INSANE, MAN, YOU

HEAR ME! GET UP! GET THE FUCK UP AND
FIGHT ME! FIGHT ME! FIGHT ME! FIGHT ME!

*Rain and sounds continue for some time. Then suddenly
stop.*

THOMAS *lies crying loudly on the ground. He stands
and roars at the town.*

*We hear Doris Day singing the beautifully lonesome,
'Time to Say Goodnight'.*

During the song, THOMAS *undresses out of his wet
clothes to his underpants.*

*His body is heavily bruised and scarred from where
he's been hurting himself.*

He lowers the light-blue suit towards him.

*He puts it on. It's a little too big and we can guess that
it's his father's suit.*

The song ends.

MAMMY (*sighing*). Ohhh, Doris Day. Sure that's Heaven
there, isn't it?

A pause.

Doris Day did for baby pink what de Valera did for
black, didn't she, Thomas. She's a real beauty.

A pause.

I'd love to have a cup of tea and a biscuit with Doris.
She doesn't look like a Jammie Dodger sort of woman
but of course that's no reason not to like her. She's
more of a Lemon Puff lady, really.

A pause.

How's the river looking, Thomas?

THOMAS. As rivers do. Different but the same.

MAMMY. Ah, that's good. Sure no news is good news.

A pause.

You're off out, are ya?

A pause.

THOMAS. The community dance is on in the school hall. I thought I'd show my face to them.

MAMMY. There's no point being locked up in here with your mammy all this time.

THOMAS. Sure I don't mind that. I don't mind that at all, Mammy.

A pause.

MAMMY. You're so good to me. I love ya, son. I really do.

THOMAS. I don't know what sort of creature I am without you, Mammy. It seems like I've nearly got it all sewn up in here. Almost. And if I wish it strong enough I can sort of see Daddy next to you on the couch watching the quiz shows on the telly… And I'd be sitting by his feet.

A pause.

Sometimes I feel that love's gone on holidays… that somehow it slipped out the front door to another place entirely, Mammy.

A pause.

I'll be home very late, I'd say. I'll be dead quiet.

MAMMY. You've something on your mind, Thomas?

THOMAS. No no. (*Slight pause.*) Sweet dreams, Mammy.

THOMAS *turns off the reel-to-reel in the kitchen. He kisses the table like he was kissing the top of her head.*

*He walks out of this space. He barely bothers with the
'locks on the door'. He steps to the outside. The street
reel-to-reel magically turns on.*

The sound of a car passing.

The sound of a dog barking.

The sound of Billy saying hello.

BILLY. Howya, Thomas!

THOMAS. I feel the front door's gentle shove behind me
as I step out into Inishfree. My town. (*Slight pause.*) I
look across the road as they queue to get inside the
hall. I watch Dwain Flynn relieve himself against our
house and I think of me tomorrow on the cold hard
ground scrubbing his memory away. (*Pause.*) I watch
Simple Eamon Moran chattin' to Timmy O'Leary
ahead of me in the queue. Timmy looks at me and I
watch him mouth the word 'Edel' and Simple Eamon
laughin'.

A pause.

Then Mrs O'Donnell and her husband come over to
join in. I watch as he replays my beating, doing the face
of a crying baba. The face of Thomas. All I can see is
the emptiness inside them. Their life scooped out from
them. Now I feel… nothing for them.

A pause.

There is a town where angels from Heaven come to
visit Earth. There's a great love between all men and
women there. A respect, a kindness. Just a light warm
wind is felt through the town as the river pops and
gurgles with ease. There are no wicked tricks played.
Words are pure. There's only goodness there.

A pause.

The queue begins its shuffle into the hall. There's so much that has to be said to these people. And I feel God's strength building me up and holding my hand as I walk... walk into Hell.

Sudden sound of the dance as colourful balloons fall onto the stage. THOMAS *walks in all hunched. Suddenly he has the confidence to do what he must do.*

THOMAS *runs up the and fires on the reel-to-reel he was working on at the very start.*

A huge cacophony of voices is heard – the voices of the people of Inishfree judging him, mocking him. This is mixed with the sound of people dancing to music. It swirls around like a storm.

THOMAS *stands on a chair and addresses them through a microphone.*

A hell of a day, hey, everyone!? A hell of day! I say ye all had a good laugh down in Boyle's tonight, didn't ya?! Laughin' about me! All the chat about Thomas Magill and his mocky-a angel! Well, it's me who's laughin' now, ya hear me! (*Slight pause.*) Dwain Flynn and your filthy mouth... you, Charlie McAnerny – throwin' shapes around town like ya own it! I see ya both there! I'm lookin' at ya and you're lookin' back at me, aren't ya?! None of your dirty words now, Dwain! My words, Charlie! My words, Mrs Cleary! Shame on you! Mr O'Donnell, the Devil's keepin' a special seat for your backside! What you did to me outside on the street?! You will burn in Hell for that?! It's me who's laughin' now at you and your wife! (*Laughs.*) The rest of ya – I did my best! My very best but that is over! I listened when no one else would listen to ya! I believed that you could all do some good but that was before you tricked me like a fool! Taking advantage of my search for love and you tricked that girl too, didn't ya?!

The Devil has had his last day in Inishfree, make no mistake! A hell of a day for him! (*Slight pause.*) What are me and Mammy and Trixie to you, hey? We are nothin'! When my daddy died and we lost the shop – you gave us no respect! You used us for all those years and then dumped us aside like old rubbish! That's right, isn't it?! Laughin' in Boyle's pub, tonight, laughin' and barkin' just like every other night! Stampin' my good name into the ground and cursin' God like the hounds that you are! You all recognise my daddy's suit, don't ya?! My daddy would smash the lot of ya if he was here in this hall! He would beat ya senseless – and it's you listenin' to me!

THOMAS *quickly gets down, puts on a pair of shabby angel wings and hops back up on the seat. He's suddenly more focused now.*

And God said to me, 'Come back up to Heaven, Thomas! Your good work has been ignored, as was my son's good work! Join your daddy! Your mammy will be saved for she is the Mother of Righteousness! Leave Inishfree, Thomas! Leave them to die!' And we will go up to Heaven and sit with the Lord God and we will make a new house up there… and I will forget you and that girl you sent to trick me! I will start each new day and night with my soul clean, my heart light, this town forgotten! It's too late to repent, by the way. It's far too late! 'For he who sows to his own flesh will from the flesh reap corruption.' I am stronger than the lot of you and I will watch you die… because you are not God's friends – you are the Devil's friends! SO… HEAR… THIS… NOW!

THOMAS *places the microphone against the tape recorder and presses the play button.*

He presses the play button on the cassette player around his neck.

We hear the voices of THOMAS *and the fourteen-year-old Edel down by the river. She speaks with an English accent.*

EDEL. Let's sit for a minute only 'cause I gotta get back. What's the time anyways?! You haven't spoken for a half-hour! Somethin' up? Thinkin' about God and things? Hello?! Anyone in there! Right, I really gotta go! I told the girls I'd be back by five to get ready for the dance...

THOMAS (*on tape*). Can I hold your hand?

A slight pause.

EDEL. No. Definitely not. Let's go!

THOMAS (*on tape*). Please, Edel!

EDEL. Are you recording this?! The girls said you would! Let me see it! Come on! Give it to me!

She is heard grabbing the microphone.

(*Shouts into the microphone.*) Hello, Thomas!! Hello! It's me! It's Edel!

THOMAS (*on tape*). Give it back...

EDEL (*continuing, pretending to be scared*). Someone help! Help – help me!

THOMAS (*on tape*). Stop that!

He grabs the microphone back.

EDEL. Fuck this, I'm off! Are you staying or what?!

THOMAS (*on tape*). I want to hold your hand, Angel!

He grabs her arm.

EDEL. OW! Don't fucking do that...!

THOMAS (*on tape*). Stay with me!

EDEL. You're hurting me…!

THOMAS (*on tape*). Don't speak to me like that!

EDEL. Let go! STOP!

THOMAS (*on tape*). Did they send you?!

EDEL. That hurts!

THOMAS (*on tape*). My God, have they sent you here… SIT DOWN!

EDEL. It was a dare, that's all! A DARE!

Edel is heard being punched hard in the face.

THOMAS (*on tape*). Out!

EDEL. Oh, Jesus, no…!

THOMAS (*on tape*). OUT, DEVIL OUT!

EDEL (*screaming*). NO, THOMAS, STOP! HELP! SOMEONE HELP ME!

THOMAS *punches her again and again.*

THOMAS (*on tape*). OUT! OUT! OUT! OUT!

A sudden horrific noise of the tape recorder smashing against her head.

(*On tape.*) Help me, God… Help me…

THOMAS *smashes her head with the tape recorder over and over and over.*

THOMAS *listens to it for some more moments until he's heard enough.*

He stops the cassette player.

Silence.

How small he looks in this huge space.

He turns to an 'imaginary good angel' and tries so hard to lose himself back in the pretend.

THOMAS. And now, good angel… I can kiss your hand.

He kisses the microphone.

Everything is so right here. Because nobody's listening. Nobody's listening. Nobody's listening. Nobody's listening. Nobody's listening…

For all his trying to escape his past… in the moment he knows the fight is lost.

His hand slowly holds the microphone out from his body. He drops it.

It smashes against the ground.

Blackout.

The End.